Red Hats
Purple Shoes
& Afternoon Teas

Recipes for When Red Hatters Gather

Printed in the United States of America
by G&R Publishing Co.

Distributed By:

507 Industrial Street
Waverly, IA 50677

ISBN 1-56383-166-X
Item #7050

Table of Contents

Finger Sandwiches *1*

Pastries *25*

Cookies & Scones *39*

Desserts *81*

Cocktails *109*

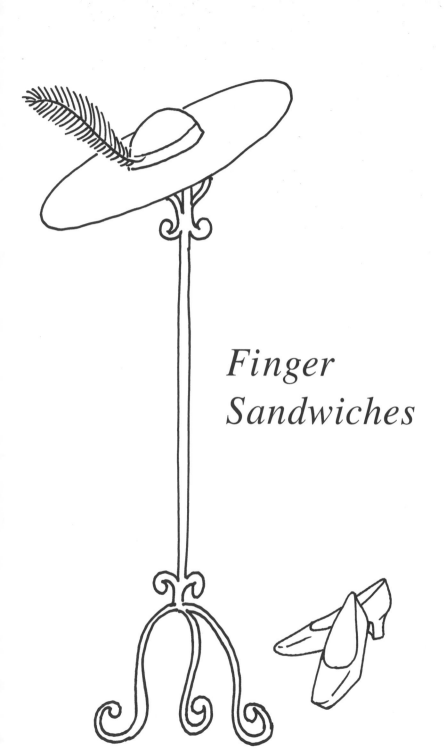

*Finger
Sandwiches*

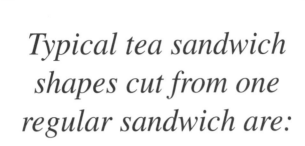

Typical tea sandwich shapes cut from one regular sandwich are:

* *four squares* ....

* *four triangles* ....

* *two rectangles* ....

* *four small oblong* ....
  rectangles

Simple, Elegant Chicken Salad Sandwiches

2 C. cooked, diced chicken
1/2 C. mayonnaise
1/2 C. sliced almonds

Salt and pepper to taste
Bread of your choice, buttered

In a medium bowl, mix diced chicken with mayonnaise and stir until well combined. Stir in sliced almonds. Salt and pepper according to taste. Refrigerate mixture until well chilled. Lightly spread filling on the top and bottom slices of bread and assemble sandwiches. Trim crusts and cut into tea sandwiches.

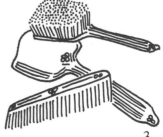

Bacon & Egg Sandwiches

4 hard cooked eggs,
    finely chopped
6 slices cooked, crisp
    bacon, crumbled
1/4 C. mayonnaise

Salt and pepper to taste
1/4 C. finely chopped
    watercress
Bread of your choice,
    buttered

In a medium bowl, mix cooked eggs, bacon and mayonnaise and stir until well combined. Salt and pepper according to taste. Spread filling on the top and bottom slices of buttered bread. Sprinkle watercress on one slice then top with the other. Trim crusts and cut into tea sandwiches.

Crunchy Chicken Salad Sandwiches

1 C. cooked chicken, finely
    chopped
1/3 C. sliced water chestnuts,
    finely chopped

1/2 C. mayonnaise
Bread of your choice,
    buttered

In a medium bowl, mix chicken, water chestnuts and mayonnaise and stir until well combined. Spread filling on the top and bottom slices of buttered bread and assemble sandwiches. Trim crusts and cut into tea sandwiches.

Fancy Tuna Salad Sandwiches

1 (6 oz.) can water packed
   tuna, drained
1/4 C. finely chopped
   red onion
1 tsp. red wine vinegar

1 hard cooked egg, chopped
1/4 C. mayonnaise
Bread of your choice,
   buttered
Alfalfa sprouts

In a medium bowl, mix tuna, onion and egg then add vinegar. Add mayonnaise and stir until well combined. Spread filling on the top and bottom slices of buttered bread. Sprinkle alfalfa sprouts on one slice then assemble sandwiches. Trim crusts and cut into tea sandwiches.

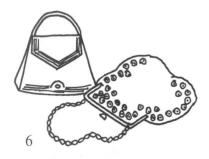

Turkey Havarti Rolls

1 tomato, chopped
1 small bunch green onion,
    chopped
Mayonnaise

4 large (12") tortillas
12 oz. sliced deli turkey
Havarti cheese, thinly sliced
1 C. alfalfa sprouts

In a small bowl, toss together chopped tomato and green onion. Set aside. Spread 1 to 2 tablespoons mayonnaise over each tortilla. Layer the turkey, cheese and alfalfa sprouts over tortillas. Sprinkle tomato and onion mixture over all then roll the tortilla tightly. Refrigerate until ready to serve. To serve, slice into 1" rounds.

Crab Salad Sandwiches

1 C. flaked crabmeat
1/4 C. chopped black olives
1/4 C. finely chopped celery

2 T. mayonnaise
1/4 C. seafood cocktail sauce
Bread of your choice, buttered

In a medium bowl, mix crabmeat, black olives, celery, mayonnaise and cocktail sauce and stir until well combined. Lightly spread filling on the top and bottom slices of buttered bread and assemble sandwiches. Trim crusts and cut into tea sandwiches.

Strawberry Delight Sandwiches

1 (8 oz.) pkg. strawberry
    cream cheese, softened
1/2 C. finely chopped walnuts,
    toasted*

Firm, ripe strawberries, halved
White bread, buttered

Spread strawberry cream cheese on the top and bottom slices of buttered bread. Sprinkle chopped walnuts over the cream cheese on one slice and assemble sandwiches. Trim crusts and cut into tea sandwiches. Using a toothpick, spear strawberry half to the top of each sandwich immediately before serving.

*To toast walnuts, place nuts in a single layer on a baking sheet. Bake at 350° for approximately 10 minutes or until nuts are golden brown.

Pineapple Nut Sandwiches

1 C. finely chopped walnuts, toasted*

1 (8 oz.) pkg. cream cheese, softened

1 (8 oz.) can crushed pineapple, well drained

Bread of your choice, buttered

In a medium bowl, mix chopped walnuts, cream cheese and crushed pineapple and stir until well combined. Lightly spread filling on the top and bottom slices of buttered bread and assemble sandwiches. Trim crusts and cut into tea sandwiches.

*To toast walnuts, place nuts in a single layer on a baking sheet. Bake at 350° for approximately 10 minutes or until nuts are golden brown.

Cucumber Tea Sandwiches

1/2 small onion, finely
   chopped
2 (8 oz.) pkgs. cream cheese,
   softened

1 large cucumber, peeled and
   thinly sliced
Bread of your choice, buttered

In a medium bowl, mix onion and cream cheese and stir until well blended. Spread 1 tablespoon cream cheese and onion mixture on bread. Arrange cucumber slices over cream cheese mixture. Serve sandwiches open-faced or closed. Trim crusts and cut into tea sandwiches.

Chicken & Pineapple Sandwiches

1 (8 oz.) can crushed pineapple,
   well drained
1 C. cooked chicken, diced

2 C. walnuts, finely chopped
1/2 C. mayonnaise
Bread of your choice, buttered

In a medium bowl, mix pineapple, chicken, walnuts and mayonnaise and stir until well combined. Spread filling on the top and bottom slices of buttered bread and assemble sandwiches. Trim crusts and cut into tea sandwiches.

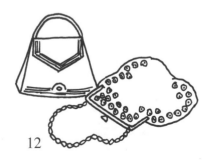

Walnut Tuna Sandwiches

1 (6 oz.) can water packed
    tuna, drained
2 T. finely chopped
    sweet pickles
1 T. finely chopped pimento
1/2 C. finely chopped walnuts

1 T. finely chopped
    green pepper
6 - 8 T. mayonnaise
1/2 tsp. salt
Bread of your choice, buttered

In a medium bowl, flake tuna then mix with sweet pickles, pimento, walnuts, green pepper, mayonnaise and salt. Stir until well combined. Spread filling on the top and bottom slices of buttered bread and assemble sandwiches. Trim crusts and cut into tea sandwiches.

13

Cucumber
Sandwiches

1/2 cucumber, peeled and
  thinly sliced
1/2 C. unsalted butter, softened
1/2 C. coarsely chopped
  watercress leaves

Salt to taste
1/2 C. alfalfa sprouts
White bread

Place cucumber slices between layers of paper towels to remove excess moisture. In a small bowl, mix butter and watercress and stir until well combined. Spread mixture on the top and bottom slices of buttered bread. Place cucumber slices onto the bottom slices and sprinkle with salt. Cover each sandwich with about a tablespoon of alfalfa sprouts and assemble sandwiches. Trim crusts and cut into tea sandwiches.

Egg Salad Sandwiches

8 hard cooked eggs,
   coarsely mashed
1/2 C. mayonnaise
Salt and pepper to taste

1 T. finely chopped
   fresh dill
Bread of your choice,
   buttered

In a medium bowl, mix eggs, mayonnaise, salt, pepper and dill and stir until well combined. Spread filling on half of the buttered bread slices. Assemble sandwiches. Trim crusts and cut into tea sandwiches.

Smoked Salmon Sandwiches

1/4 C. mayonnaise
1 T. minced green onion
1 T. minced fresh dill weed
1 tsp. prepared horseradish
Pepper to taste

4 pieces smoked salmon
12 thin cucumber slices
2 teaspoons butter, softened
8 slices pumpernickel bread

In a small bowl, mix mayonnaise, green onion, dill weed, horseradish and pepper and stir until well combined. Set aside. Spread butter thinly over pumpernickel bread slices then spread mayonnaise mixture on each bread slice. Divide salmon and cucumber slices evenly between half of the bread slices then assemble sandwiches. Trim crusts and cut into tea sandwiches.

Almond Chicken Salad

2 whole chicken breasts,
    cooked and finely chopped
1/4 C. finely chopped almonds
2 tsp. fresh lemon juice
2 T. fresh chopped parsley

4 celery stalks, finely chopped
Salt to taste
Mayonnaise to moisten
Bread of your choice, buttered

In a large bowl, mix chicken, almonds, lemon juice, parsley, celery, salt and enough mayonnaise to moisten the mixture. Stir until well combined. Spread filling over half of the buttered bread slices and assemble sandwiches. Trim crusts and cut into tea sandwiches.

Cranberry
Fingers

Whole cranberry sauce
Dijon mustard

Thinly sliced smoked turkey
Bread of your choice, buttered

In a medium bowl, mix some Dijon mustard in with whole cranberry sauce, flavor to your tastes. Stir until well combined. Spread mixture on the top and bottom slices of buttered bread then add a small thin slice of smoked turkey. Assemble sandwiches. Trim crusts and cut into tea sandwiches.

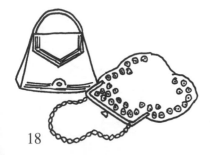

Celery-Nut Sandwiches

1 (8 oz.) pkg. cream cheese,
    softened
1/4 C. milk

1/2 C. celery
1/2 C. chopped walnuts
Bread of your choice

In a medium bowl, beat together cream cheese and milk until well mixed. Add celery and walnuts. Spread filling on the top and bottom slices of buttered bread. Assemble sandwiches. Trim crusts and cut into tea sandwiches.

Pineapple Cream Sandwiches

1 (8 oz.) pkg. cream cheese, softened
1/4 C. milk

1 C. crushed pineapple, drained well
Boston brown bread

In a small bowl, beat together cream cheese and milk until well mixed. Add crushed pineapple and stir until combined. Spread filling on the top and bottom slices of buttered bread. Assemble sandwiches. Trim crusts and cut into tea sandwiches.

Apricot Ham Finger Sandwiches

2 (8 oz.) pkgs. cream cheese,
    softened
1/3 C. apricot preserves
Thinly sliced ham

Bread of your choice,
    buttered
Dried apricots, quartered
    into slivers

In a medium bowl, beat together cream cheese and apricot preserves until well mixed. Spread mixture on the top and bottom slices of buttered bread. Add a small slice of ham to half of the bread slices then assemble sandwiches. Trim crusts and cut into tea sandwiches. Top each sandwich with an apricots sliver.

Beef and Cheddar Rolls

Mayonnaise
4 large (12") tortillas
12 oz. sliced roast beef

Cheddar cheese, thinly sliced
1/2 head iceberg lettuce
3 Roma tomatoes, thinly sliced

Spread 1 to 2 tablespoons mayonnaise over each tortilla. Layer the remaining ingredients over the tortilla beginning with the roast beef and ending with thinly sliced tomatoes. Roll tortillas tightly and refrigerate until ready to serve. To serve, slice into 1" rounds.

Turkey Orange Sandwiches

Thinly sliced roasted
  turkey breast
Orange marmalade

Rye bread, buttered
Mandarin orange slices,
  optional

Place turkey on both slices of buttered bread. Lightly spread marmalade over one of the turkey slices and assemble sandwiches. Trim crust and cut into tea sandwiches. If desired, using a toothpick, spear an orange slice to the top of each sandwich immediately before serving.

Parsley, Olive &
Tuna Salad Rolls

2 (6 oz.) cans water packed tuna, well drained
1/2 C. mayonnaise
2 tsp. fresh lemon juice
3 T. fresh minced parsley
1/3 C. chopped green olives
1/4 C. grated parmesan cheese
1 head green leaf lettuce
4 (12") tortillas

In a medium bowl, mix drained tuna, mayonnaise, lemon juice, parsley, green olives and parmesan cheese and stir until well combined. Arrange leaf lettuce over tortillas to cover. Spread mixture over leaf lettuce then roll the tortilla tightly. Refrigerate until ready to serve. To serve, slice into 1" rounds.

Olive Pecan Cream Sandwiches

1 (8 oz.) pkg. cream cheese, softened
1/2 C. mayonnaise
1/2 C. finely chopped pecans
1 C. chopped green olives
Dash of pepper
Bread of choice, buttered

In a medium bowl, beat cream cheese and mayonnaise until smooth. Stir in chopped pecans, green olives and pepper. Mix until well combined. Cover and refrigerate overnight. Remove from refrigerator and let set for 1 hour before using. Spread filling over the top and bottom slices of buttered bread. Assemble sandwiches. Trim crusts and cut into tea sandwiches.

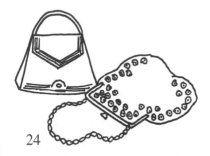

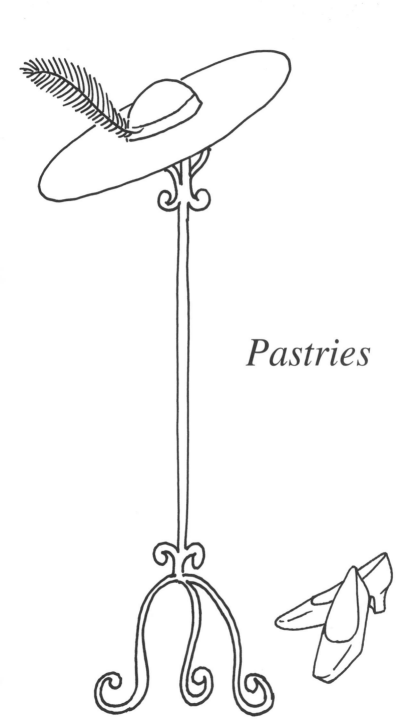

Pastries

Danish Puff

1 C. flour, sifted
1/2 C. butter or margarine,
   softened
2 T. water
1/2 C. butter
1 C. water

1 tsp. almond flavoring
1 C. flour, sifted
3 eggs
Powdered sugar icing
Slivered almonds

Preheat oven to 350°. In a medium bowl, add 1 cup sifted flour, cut in 1/2 cup butter and sprinkle 2 tablespoons water over crumb mixture. Mix all with fork. Shape dough into a ball and divide in half. Pat each piece of dough into 3 x 12" strips. Place strips 3" apart on an ungreased baking sheet. In a saucepan, mix 1/2 cup butter and 1 cup water. Bring to a boil. Remove from heat and add almond flavoring. Beat in 1 cup flour, stirring quickly to prevent lumping. When smooth add 1 egg at a time, beating well after each until smooth. Divide mixture in half and spread evenly over each pastry strip. Bake for 60 minutes or until top is crisp and browned. Puff will shrink while cooking leaving a custardy portion in the center. When cooled, frost with powdered sugar icing and sprinkle with slivered almonds.

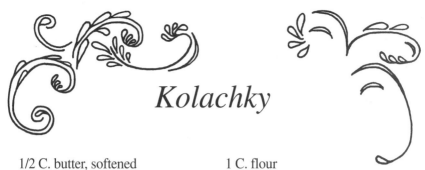

Kolachky

1/2 C. butter, softened
4 oz. cream cheese,
    softened

1 C. flour
Assorted fruit preserves

In a large bowl, beat butter and cream cheese until smooth and creamy. Gradually add flour, mixing until a soft dough forms. Divide dough into 2 equal parts, cover and chill until firm. Preheat oven to 375°. On a floured surface, roll dough out to 1/8" thickness. Cut into 3" squares. Place 1 teaspoon preserves in the center of each square. Bring 2 opposite corners together. Pinch tightly to seal then fold pinched edge to one side. Place 1" apart on an ungreased baking sheet. Bake for 10 to 15 minutes or until lightly browned.

Peach Tart Tatin

2/3 C. sugar
3 T. water
2 tsp. light corn syrup
2 T. butter
1 tsp. fresh lemon juice

5 medium unpeeled peaches,
    pitted and quartered
1 (1/2 of a 17.3 oz. pkg.)
    sheet frozen puff
    pastry, thawed
Whipped cream, optional

Preheat oven to 375°. In a small skillet over medium heat, mix sugar, water and corn syrup and stir until sugar dissolves. Increase heat and let boil without stirring until syrup is a deep amber color, about 7 minutes. Remove from heat and quickly stir in butter and lemon juice. Pour caramel into a greased 9" round baking pan with 1 1/2" high sides. Place peaches, skin side down, over caramel mixture, covering completely. Bake for 30 minutes or until peaches are just tender. On a floured surface, roll out pastry to a 12" square. Using a 10" round pan as a pattern, cut out a round piece of pastry. Pierce all over with a fork and place over peaches, pressing around peaches on sides. Bake for 25 to 30 minutes or until pastry is puffed and golden. Let cool for 5 minutes. Run knife around the pan edge. Invert onto a serving platter and cut into thin wedges. If desired, serve with whipped cream.

Chocolate Croissants

1 tube crescent roll dough   Semisweet chocolate chips

Preheat oven to 375°. On a floured surface, slightly roll individual dough triangles to spread out but not flatten. At the broad end of each triangle, place a tablespoon of chocolate chips. Roll each triangle into a crescent being careful not to let the chips fall out. Place each on a greased baking sheet. Bake for 12 to 14 minutes. Other variations to this recipe include different types of chips, nuts or butter and cinnamon sugar.

Fruit Crostata

1 1/4 C. flour	4 medium plums or 2 medium
1/3 C. sugar	peaches, pitted and cut
1/4 tsp. salt	into 1/2" pieces
1/2 C. butter,	1/2 C. raspberries or
softened	blueberries
1 egg yolk	2 T. sugar
1/4 C. raspberry or other jam	1 T. flour

In a medium bowl, whisk together 1 1/4 cup flour, 1/3 cup sugar and salt. Cut in butter until the mixture resembles fine crumbs. Using a spatula, stir in egg yolk until the dough forms a ball. If too sticky, may refrigerate for 30 minutes. Preheat oven to 375°. On a lightly floured surface, roll dough into an 11" circle. Place on a greased baking sheet. Spread jam over top leaving a 1" border. Toss together fruit, 2 tablespoons sugar and 1 tablespoon flour and distribute evenly over jam. Bake for 30 minutes.

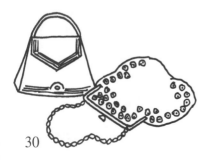

Scottish Shortbread

3/4 C. butter, softened   1 1/2 T. sugar
1/4 C. powdered sugar   1 1/2 C. flour

Preheat oven to 300°. In a medium bowl, beat butter and sugar on medium speed until very fluffy. Mixing on low speed, gradually add flour, mixing until well blended and smooth. Be careful not to over mix. Press dough into a greased 8" square pan and pierce all over with a fork. Bake for 45 minutes or until a toothpick inserted in the center comes out clean. Cut into small rectangles while still warm.

Cream Puffs

1/2 C. water
1/2 C. whole milk
1/2 C. butter
1 C. flour
4 eggs

Vanilla pudding
8 oz. (1 C.) bittersweet
    chocolate
1/2 C. heavy cream
2 T. butter

In a saucepan over medium heat, mix water, milk and butter and bring to a boil. Add 1 cup flour and stir vigorously with a wooden spoon until the mixture pulls away from the sides of the pan. Continue to cook, stirring frequently for a minute longer. Transfer to a mixing bowl and let cool for 6 to 8 minutes. Beat in eggs, one at a time, on low speed until dough is smooth and shiny. Allow dough to cool for 10 minutes or up to 4 hours in the refrigerator. Preheat oven to 400°. Using a heaping tablespoon, spoon balls of dough onto a greased baking sheet. Bake for 15 minutes then reduce oven temperature to 350° and bake for an additional 10 to 15 minutes until puffs are golden brown and firm. If undercooked, puffs will collapse when removed from the oven. Once cooled, slice off tops to expose the hollow center. Fill centers with vanilla pudding. In a double boiler, melt chocolate, cream and butter. Allow mixture to cool slightly then spoon over the tops of cream puffs. Refrigerate until ready to serve.

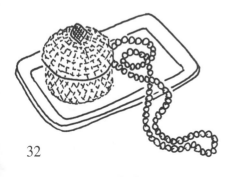

White Chocolate Cranberry Pear Pastry

1 (17.25 oz.) pkg. frozen
    puff pastry sheets (2 sheets)
1 egg
1 T. water
1 (6 oz.) pkg. white baking
    chocolate, divided

2 (15 oz.) cans sliced pears,
    well drained
1/4 C. dried cranberries
Water

Thaw pastry sheets for 30 minutes at room temperature. Preheat oven to 375°. On a lightly floured surface, lay out pastry sheets. Trim about 1" off each corner of each pastry sheet. Reserve trimmings for decoration, if desired. Place 1 pastry sheet on an ungreased baking sheet. Chop 6 squares of the white chocolate. Mix chopped chocolate, pears and cranberries. Spread mixture over the pastry on baking sheet to within 1" of edges. In a small bowl, beat egg and 1 tablespoon water. Brush pastry edges with egg mixture. Top filled pastry with remaining sheet. Press edges together with a fork to seal. Roll out reserved pastry and use a cookie cutter to cut out decorations for pastry top, if desired. Brush entire pastry with egg mixture. Cut several 2" slits, 2" apart in pastry top. Bake for 35 minutes or until pastry is golden. Cool for 30 minutes. Melt remaining 2 squares white chocolate and drizzle over pastry.

Lemon Curd
Tartlets

2 whole eggs
2 egg yolks
1/2 C. sugar
1/3 C. fresh lemon juice
1/4 C. butter

2 T. sugar
1 C. flour
1/2 C. shortening
2 - 3 T. ice water

In a double boiler, combine eggs and yolks and lightly beat. Mix in 1/2 cup sugar and lemon juice. Cook over simmering heat for 5 minutes, stirring constantly, until mixture thickens slightly. Remove from heat and stir in butter until melted. Chill. Preheat oven to 375°. For tartlet crust, in a medium bowl, mix 2 tablespoons sugar and flour. Cut in shortening until mixture resembles fine crumbs. Stir in 2 to 3 tablespoons ice water and knead briefly by hand until mixture forms a ball. Split dough into 24 small balls and press each over the bottom and up the sides of a mini muffin cup. Prick holes on the bottom of dough. Bake for 12 to 18 minutes. Let cool completely then fill with chilled lemon curd.

Apple Pastry

2 C. flour
1/2 tsp. salt
1/4 C. shortening
1/4 C. butter, softened
3 T. ice water
1 1/2 lbs. cooking apples,
    cored, peeled and sliced

5 T. sugar, divided
1 T. butter
1 tsp. lemon zest
3 - 4 T. water
Cold water

In a medium bowl, combine flour and salt. Cut in shortening and 1/4 cup butter until the mixture resembles fine crumbs. Sprinkle 3 tablespoons ice water over all and blend with a fork. Gather dough into a ball and knead lightly for a few seconds to form a smooth dough. Cover or wrap in plastic wrap and chill for at least 30 minutes. For the filling, mix the apples, 4 tablespoons sugar, 1 tablespoon butter, zest and 3 to 4 tablespoons water in a saucepan. Cook, covered, over low heat until apples are soft. While warm, slightly mash. Preheat oven to 400°. On a lightly floured surface, roll pasty into a 12" square. Spread filling over half of the pastry leaving a 1/2" border. Brush the exposed border with cold water then fold pastry over the filling and pinch edges together. Slide onto a greased baking sheet. Brush pastry top with cold water and cut 2 or 3 one inch slits in the top. Sprinkle remaining sugar over all. Bake for 20 to 25 minutes.

Apricot Shortcakes

1 1/2 C. flour
3/4 C. butter, softened
1/3 C. rice flour
1/3 C. powdered sugar

5 T. apricot jam
Apricot jam
Powdered sugar

Preheat oven to 375°. In a medium bowl, cut butter into flour until the mixture resembles fine crumbs. Add rice flour and powdered sugar and stir until well combined. Make a well in the center and add 5 tablespoons jam. Work the dough until all ingredients are well blended and the dough is smooth. On a lightly floured surface, roll dough to a 3/4" thickness. Cut into fancy shapes and place on a greased baking sheet. Make a small hallow in the center of each shortcake and put a scant teaspoon of jam in each. Bake for 20 minutes. When cooled, lightly dust each shortcake with powdered sugar.

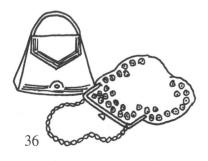

Fruit Turnovers

2 C. flour
3 T. powdered sugar
1/2 tsp. salt
3/4 C. butter, softened
1 egg

1 egg yolk
Preserves or pie filling
1 egg, beaten
Sugar

In a medium bowl, combine flour, powdered sugar and salt. Cut in butter until mixture resembles fine crumbs. In a separate bowl, beat together egg and egg yolk. Add to crumb mixture and stir until well combined. Form dough into a ball and knead or a few seconds until smooth. Cover with plastic wrap and chill for at least 30 minutes. Preheat oven to 400°. On a lightly floured surface, roll dough to a 1/4" thickness. Cut out 3" diameter circles. Spoon your choice of preserves or pie filling into the center of each. Brush edges of each circle with lightly beaten egg then fold dough over. Pinch edges together or crimp with a fork. Place each turnover on a lightly greased baking sheet. Brush tops with egg and sprinkle with sugar. Cut 2 small slits in each pastry to allow steam to escape. Bake for 20 to 25 minutes.

Gobbet Cakes

1/2 C. butter, softened
1/2 C. sugar
1 tsp. lemon zest
3/4 C. flour
2 tsp. baking powder

2 eggs, beaten
2 - 3 T. fresh lemon juice
(1 lemon)
Candied ginger

Preheat oven to 375°. In a large bowl, cream butter and sugar with lemon zest. In a separate bowl, mix flour and baking powder. Stir eggs into the sugar mixture then gradually fold flour mixture in. Stir in lemon juice. The batter will be thick for a dropping consistency. Drop by heaping teaspoonfuls into greased mini muffin tins. Place a small piece of candied ginger on the top of each cake. Bake for 12 to 15 minutes.

Cookies
& Scones

Danish Oatmeal Cookies

1/4 C. butter, softened
1/4 C. margarine, softened
1/2 C. powdered sugar
1 tsp. vanilla
1/2 C. flour

1/4 tsp. salt
1/2 C. quick oats
1/2 C. chopped walnuts
   or pecans
Powdered sugar, optional

Preheat oven to 325°. Cream the butter, margarine and powdered sugar. Add vanilla. Sift together the flour and salt then stir into creamed mixture. Stir in the oats and nuts. Drop teaspoonfuls onto an ungreased cookie sheet. Bake for 20 minutes or until lightly browned. If desired, sift additional powdered sugar over partly cooled cookies.

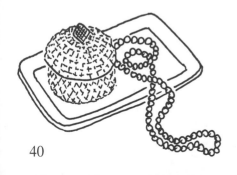

Gingersnap Cookies

3/4 C. margarine, softened
1 C. packed brown sugar
1/4 C. molasses
1 egg
2 1/4 C. flour
1 tsp. ginger

1 tsp. cinnamon
1/2 tsp. cloves
2 tsp. baking soda
1/4 tsp. salt
Sugar

Preheat oven to 375°. Cream shortening and brown sugar with a mixer until sugar crystals are dissolved. Beat in molasses and egg. Sift the dry ingredients together in a medium bowl then add to the creamed mixture. Stir until well mixed. Roll dough into walnut sized balls. Roll dough balls into sugar and place on a greased cookie sheet. Bake for 10 to 13 minutes.

Cream Scones

2 C. flour
2 tsp. baking powder
2 T. sugar
1/2 tsp. salt
6 T. butter, softened

2 eggs, well beaten
1/2 C. plus 1 T. heavy
cream, divided
Coarse sugar crystals

Preheat oven to 425°. Sift flour, baking powder, sugar and salt into a medium bowl. Cut in butter until the mixture resembles coarse crumbs. Make a well in the center of the crumb mixture and add beaten eggs and 1/2 cup cream. Mix until dough begins to form a ball then knead dough with your hands in the bowl for 30 seconds. Be careful not to over knead. Place dough on a lightly floured surface and divide in half. Form each half into a ball and flatten to form a circle about 3/4" thick and 5" in diameter. Cut each circle into 8 wedges. Place wedges 1" apart on a lightly greased baking sheet. Brush tops of wedges with remaining cream then sprinkle each wedge with sugar crystals. Bake in for 12 to 15 minutes.

Cranberry Drops

1/2 C. butter or margarine,
    softened
1 C. sugar
3/4 C. packed brown sugar
1/4 C. whole milk
2 T. orange juice
1 egg

3 C. flour
1 tsp. baking powder
1/2 tsp. salt
1/4 tsp. baking soda
1 C. chopped walnuts
2 1/2 C. cranberries, coarsely
    chopped

Preheat oven to 375°. In a large bowl, cream butter, sugar and brown sugar until fluffy. Add milk, orange juice and egg and stir until combined. In a separate bowl, stir together flour, baking powder, salt and baking soda until well blended. Add to creamed mixture and stir until well blended. Stir in nuts and cranberries. Drop dough by teaspoonfuls onto a greased baking sheet. Bake for 12 to 14 minutes.

Cream Cheese Cookies

1 C. butter, softened
4 oz. cream cheese, softened
1 C. sugar
1 egg yolk, at room temperature

1 tsp. vanilla
2 1/2 C. flour
3/4 tsp. salt

Preheat oven to 325°. In a medium bowl, mix butter, cream cheese and sugar until well combined. Stir in egg yolk and vanilla. Add flour and salt and mix until well combined. Form dough into 1" balls. Place dough balls on an ungreased cookie sheet. Flatten each ball using your hand or the bottom of a glass. Bake for 14 to 16 minutes or until golden brown.

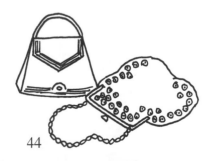

Cinnamon Hazelnut Biscotti

3/4 C. butter
1 C. sugar
2 eggs
1 1/2 tsp. vanilla
2 1/2 C. flour

1 tsp. cinnamon
3/4 tsp. baking powder
1/2 tsp. salt
1 C. hazelnuts

Preheat oven to 350°. In a medium bowl, cream together butter and sugar until light and fluffy. Beat in eggs and vanilla. Sift together flour, cinnamon, baking powder and salt and mix into the egg mixture. Stir in the hazelnuts. Shape dough into two equal logs approximately 12". Place logs on a greased baking sheet and flatten out to approximately 1/2" thickness. Bake for 30 minutes or until edges are golden and the center is firm. Remove from the oven and let cool on the pan. When loaves are cool enough to handle, use a serrated knife to slice the loaves diagonally into 1/2" thick slices. Return slices to the baking sheet. Bake for an additional 10 minutes, turning over once after 5 minutes. Cool completely and store in an airtight container.

Brownie Biscotti

1/3 C. butter, softened
2/3 C. sugar
2 eggs
1 tsp. vanilla
1 3/4 C. flour
1/3 C. unsweetened
    cocoa powder

2 tsp. baking powder
1/2 C. miniature semisweet
    chocolate chips
1/4 C. chopped walnuts
1 egg yolk, beaten
1 T. water

Preheat oven to 375°. In a large bowl, cream together the butter and sugar until smooth. Beat in the eggs one at a time then stir in vanilla. Combine the flour, cocoa and baking powder. Stir into the creamed mixture until well blended. Dough will be stiff and you may need to mix the last bit by hand. Mix in the chocolate chips and walnuts. Divide dough into 2 equal logs. Shape logs in to 9 x 2" loaves. Place loaves 4" apart onto greased baking sheet and flatten until approximately 1" thick. Brush with mixture of water and yolk. Bake for 20 to 25 minutes or until firm. Cool on baking sheet for 30 minutes then, using a serrated knife, slice the loaves diagonally into 1" slices. Return the slices to the baking sheet and bake for an additional 10 to 15 minutes on each side or until dry. Cool completely and store in an airtight container.

Lemon Sugar
Tea Cookies

3/4 C. butter
1 C. sugar
1 egg
2 T. corn syrup
1 tsp. lemon extract

2 C. flour
1 tsp. baking soda
1 tsp. baking powder
Sugar

In a medium bowl, cream together butter and 1 cup sugar until light and fluffy. Beat in egg, corn syrup and lemon extract. Stir in flour, baking soda and baking powder. Cover dough and chill in the refrigerator for at least 1 hour. Preheat oven to 325°. Shape chilled dough into walnut sized balls and roll in sugar. Place dough balls onto a greased baking sheet. Bake for 12 minutes.

Coffee House
Scones

1 C. sour cream	1/4 tsp. cream of tartar
1 tsp. baking soda	1 tsp. salt
4 C. flour	1 C. butter
1 C. sugar	1 egg
2 tsp. baking powder	1 C. raisins, optional

Preheat oven to 350°. In a small bowl, blend the sour cream and baking soda. Set aside. In a large bowl, mix the flour, sugar, baking powder, cream of tartar and salt. Cut in the butter until the mixture resembles coarse crumbs. Stir the sour cream mixture and egg into the flour mixture until just moistened. Stir in raisins. Turn dough out onto a lightly floured surface and knead briefly. Roll dough into a 3/4" thick circle. Cut into 12 wedges and place them 2" apart onto a lightly greased baking sheet. Bake for 12 to 15 minutes or until golden brown on the bottom.

Chocolate Chip Scones

2 C. flour
1/3 C. packed brown sugar
1 1/2 tsp. baking powder
1/2 tsp. baking soda
1/4 tsp. salt
6 T. unsalted butter,
    chilled and cubed

1/2 C. buttermilk
1 egg
1 1/2 tsp. almond extract
3/4 C. miniature chocolate
    chips

Preheat oven to 400°. In a large bowl, stir together flour, brown sugar, baking powder, baking soda and salt. Cut in the butter cubes using a pastry blender, two forks or a wire whisk until the mixture resembles coarse crumbs. Stir together buttermilk, egg and almond extract. Add to the flour mixture and stir until well blended. Stir in the chocolate chips. The dough will be sticky. Spread the dough into an 8" diameter circle on a lightly greased baking sheet. Cut dough with a serrated knife into 8 wedges. Bake for 17 to 19 minutes or until the top is lightly browned and place on a greased baking sheet.

Walnut Raisin Scones

2 C. flour
2 T. sugar
2 tsp. baking powder
1/2 tsp. baking soda
1/2 tsp. salt
1 T. lemon zest
1/2 C. butter, chilled and cubed

3/4 C. chopped walnuts
1/2 C. raisins
3/4 C. buttermilk
2 T. buttermilk
2 T. sugar
2 T. chopped walnuts

Preheat oven to 425°. In a large bowl, combine flour, sugar, baking powder, baking soda, salt and zest. With a pastry blender, two knives or a wire whisk, cut in butter until mixture resembles coarse crumbs. Stir in 3/4 cup walnuts and raisins. Mix in buttermilk with a fork. Gather dough into a ball and knead for 2 minutes on a lightly floured surface. Roll out to 3/4" thickness. With a chef's knife, cut into 3" triangles. Place triangles 1" apart on a greased baking sheet. Brush tops with remaining buttermilk and sprinkle with remaining sugar and walnuts. Bake for 15 minutes or until browned. Cool completely and store in an airtight container.

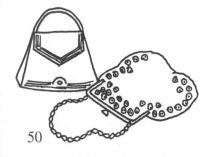

Butter Pecan Rounds

2 T. butter
1 1/2 C. chopped pecans
1 1/2 T. sugar
1/2 C. unsalted butter,
    softened
1/2 C. sugar

1/2 C. packed brown sugar
1 egg
1 tsp. vanilla
1 2/3 C. flour
1/2 tsp. baking soda
1/2 tsp. salt

Preheat oven to 350°. In a skillet over medium heat toast the pecans with 2 tablespoons butter, cooking for about 5 minutes. Sprinkle 1 1/2 tablespoons sugar over pecans. In a medium bowl, cream 1/2 cup butter with 1/2 cup sugar and brown sugar. Beat in the egg and vanilla. Mix in the flour, baking soda and salt. Stir in the pecan mixture. Drop tablespoonfuls of dough onto greased baking sheets. Bake for 10 to 12 minutes until golden brown.

Oatmeal Raisin Cookies

3 eggs, beaten
1 C. raisins
1 tsp. vanilla
1 C. butter
1 C. packed brown
   sugar

1 C. sugar
2 1/2 C. flour
1 tsp. cinnamon
2 tsp. baking soda
2 C. rolled oats
1 C. chopped pecans

In a small bowl, combine eggs, raisins and vanilla. Cover and let stand for 1 hour. Preheat oven to 350°. In a large bowl, cream butter, brown sugar and sugar together. Sift together flour, cinnamon and baking soda. Stir into the creamed mixture. Stir in raisin mixture, oats and pecans. Drop by teaspoonfuls onto an ungreased baking sheet. Bake for 10 minutes or until lightly browned.

Oatmeal Toffee Cookies

3/4 C. butter, softened
1/2 C. packed brown sugar
1 egg
1 tsp. vanilla
1 C. flour

1/2 tsp. baking soda
1/2 tsp. salt
1 1/2 C. oats
1/2 C. chopped pecans
2 C. toffee baking bits

Preheat oven to 300°. In a medium bowl, cream together the butter and brown sugar. Stir in the egg and vanilla until smooth. Sift together flour, baking soda and salt. Mix into the creamed mixture. Stir in oats, pecans and toffee bits. Drop dough by rounded tablespoons onto greased baking sheets and flatten slightly. Bake for 10 to 18 minutes. Cookies will have a dry appearance.

Pecan Filled Cookies

1/2 C. butter, softened
1 C. packed brown sugar
1 egg
1 tsp. vanilla
2 C. flour

1/2 tsp. baking soda
1/4 tsp. salt
1/2 C. chopped pecans
2 T. sour cream
1/4 C. packed brown sugar

Preheat oven to 350°. In a medium bowl, cream together the butter and 1 cup brown sugar until smooth. Beat in the egg then stir in vanilla. Combine the flour, baking soda and salt. Stir into the sugar mixture. Roll dough into 1" balls and place 2" apart onto greased baking sheets. Make a deep thumb depression in the center of each ball. Mix together the pecans, sour cream and 1/4 cup brown sugar. Fill each depression with the mixture. Bake for 8 to 11 minutes or until light brown.

Shortbread Chocolate Chip Cookies

1 3/4 C. flour
1/2 tsp. baking powder
1/4 tsp. salt
1 C. unsalted butter, softened

1/2 C. sugar
3/4 C. semisweet chocolate chips
1/2 C. chopped walnuts

Preheat oven to 300°. Sift together the flour, baking powder and salt. Set aside. In a medium bowl, cream the butter and sugar until fluffy. Gradually stir in the dry mixture then stir in the chocolate chips and walnuts. Shape dough into walnut sized balls. Place dough balls onto ungreased baking sheets 1 1/2" apart. Flatten cookies slightly. Bake for 15 to 20 minutes or until light golden brown.

Biscotti Toscani

1/3 C. butter	2 1/4 C. flour
3/4 C. sugar	1 1/2 tsp. baking powder
2 eggs	1/8 tsp. nutmeg
1 tsp. vanilla	1/4 tsp. salt
1/4 tsp. almond extract	1 C. semisweet chocolate chips
2 tsp. orange zest	1/2 C. almond pieces, toasted*

Preheat oven to 325°. In a large bowl, cream butter and sugar until light and fluffy. Beat in eggs, vanilla, almond extract and zest. Combine flour, baking powder, nutmeg and salt then stir into the creamed mixture until just blended. Stir in almonds. Divide dough into two logs. Form logs about 12" long and flatten to a 1/2" thickness. Place loaves 2" apart onto a greased and floured baking sheet. Bake for 25 minutes or until light golden brown. Cool on a wire rack for 5 minutes. With a serrated knife, cut diagonally into approximately 1/2" thick slices. Place slices back onto baking sheet and bake for an additional 10 minutes, turning over once after 5 minutes. Transfer to a wire rack to cool. Melt chocolate chips in the microwave, stirring every 20 to 30 seconds until smooth. Spread chocolate onto tops of each cookie. Cool completely and store in an airtight container.

*To toast almonds, place nuts in a single layer on a baking sheet. Bake at 350° for approximately 10 minutes or until nuts are golden brown.

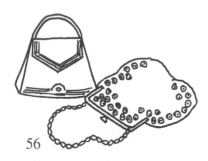

Raspberry and Almond Shortbread Thumbprints

1 C. butter, softened
2/3 C. sugar
1/2 tsp. almond extract
2 C. flour

1/2 C. seedless raspberry jam
1/2 C. powdered sugar
3/4 tsp. almond extract
1 T. milk

Preheat oven to 350°. In a medium bowl, cream together butter and sugar until smooth. Mix in 1/2 teaspoon almond extract. Mix in flour until dough comes together. Roll dough into 1 1/2" balls and place on an ungreased baking sheet. Using your thumb, make a small hole in the center of each ball. Fill each hole with jam. Bake for 14 to 18 minutes or until lightly browned. Let cool for 1 minute on baking sheet. In a medium bowl, mix powder sugar, 3/4 teaspoon almond extract and milk until smooth. Drizzle lightly over warm cookies.

Lemon Chewy Crisps

1/2 C. butter, softened
3/4 C. sugar
1 egg
1 T. lemon zest
1 1/2 tsp. fresh lemon juice

3/4 tsp. vanilla
1/2 tsp. baking powder
1/4 tsp. baking soda
1 1/4 C. flour
1/2 C. sliced almonds or
    1/4 C. sugar

Preheat oven to 350°. In a large bowl, beat butter and sugar until light and fluffy. Beat in egg, lemon zest, lemon juice, vanilla, baking powder and baking soda until well blended. On low speed, beat in flour just until blended. Drop dough by rounded teaspoonfuls 1 1/2" apart onto an ungreased baking sheet. Sprinkle with almonds or sugar. Bake for 10 to 12 minutes or until edges are lightly browned.

Orange Almond Biscotti

2 1/4 C. flour
1 1/4 C. sugar
1 pinch salt
2 tsp. baking powder
1/2 C. sliced almonds

1 T. orange zest
3 eggs, beaten
1 T. vegetable oil
1/4 tsp. almond extract

Preheat oven to 350°. In a large bowl, mix flour, sugar, baking powder, salt, almonds and orange zest until well blended. Make a well in the center and add eggs, oil and almond extract. Stir by hand until mixture forms a ball. Separate dough into 2 logs about 8" long and flatten to 3/4" thickness. Place on a greased and floured baking sheet. Bake for 20 to 25 minutes. Cool slightly. Using a serrated knife, cut diagonally into 1/2" slices. Place slices on baking sheet and bake for an additional 10 to 15 minutes, turning over after 5 to 7 minutes.

Cinnamon Drops

1 C. butter
2/3 C. sugar
1/3 C. packed brown sugar
1 egg yolk
2 C. flour

1 1/4 tsp. cinnamon
1/2 tsp. salt
1 C. chopped walnuts,
    optional

Preheat oven to 300°. In a medium bowl, cream the butter, sugar and brown sugar. Add the egg yolk and stir until well blended. In a separate bowl, mix the flour, cinnamon and salt. Add to the creamed mixture and blend well. Stir in walnuts. Drop the dough by rounded teaspoonfuls onto an ungreased cookie sheet leaving 2" between cookies. Flatten each cookie with a fork dipped in flour, pressing the dough once in each direction to make a criss-cross. Bake for 20 to 25 minutes.

Chocolate Linzer Cookies

1 1/2 C. butter	6 T. unsweetened
3/4 C. sugar	cocoa powder
1 egg	Raspberry jam
1 tsp. vanilla	Powdered sugar
3 C. flour	

In a large bowl, cream the butter and sugar until light and fluffy. Stir in the egg and vanilla. In a separate bowl, mix flour and cocoa then add to the creamed mixture and mix until well blended. Divide the dough in half then wrap each half in plastic wrap and refrigerate for 2 to 3 hours or until firm enough to roll out. Preheat oven to 350°. Roll out half of the dough at a time on a floured surface to 1/8" thick. Cut the dough with cookie cutter 3" in diameter. Cut a 1" diameter round from the center of half of the 3" rounds. Transfer cookies to a greased baking sheet. Bake for 10 minutes. Allow cookies to cool then spread raspberry jam on whole cookies. Cover each with a cut-out cookie. Sprinkle each with powdered sugar.

Iced Molasses Cookies

5 T. butter
1/4 C. sugar
1/4 C. packed brown sugar
1/2 C. molasses
1 egg
1 tsp. vanilla
1/4 C. water

2 C. flour
2 tsp. baking soda
1/4 tsp. salt
2 tsp. orange or lemon zest
2 C. powdered sugar
3 T. hot milk
2 tsp. vanilla

Preheat oven to 350°. In a heavy saucepan, melt butter, sugar, brown sugar and molasses over low heat, stirring constantly until sugars are dissolved. Remove from heat and cool then add egg, vanilla and water and stir until well blended. In a separate bowl, mix flour, baking soda, salt and zest. Add to the sugar mixture. Drop the dough by rounded teaspoonfuls onto a greased baking sheet, leaving 2" between each cookie. Bake for 10 minutes. Combine powdered sugar, hot milk and vanilla until smooth. Spread or drizzle over cooled cookies.

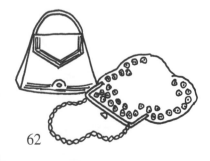

Linzer Cookies

3/4 C. butter, softened
1 C. sugar
2 eggs
1 tsp. vanilla
2 1/2 C. flour

1 tsp. baking powder
1/2 tsp. salt
Raspberry jam
Powdered Sugar

In a large bowl, cream the butter and sugar until light and fluffy. Stir in the eggs and vanilla. In a separate bowl, mix flour, baking powder and salt then add to the creamed mixture and mix until well blended. Divide the dough in half then wrap each half in plastic wrap and refrigerate for 2 to 3 hours or until firm enough to roll out. Preheat oven to 350°. Roll out half of the dough at a time on a floured surface to 1/8" thick. Cut the dough with cookie cutter 3" in diameter. Cut a 1" diameter round from the center of half of the 3" rounds. Transfer cookies to a greased baking sheet. Bake for 10 to 12 minutes watching carefully to prevent over-done cookies. Allow cookies to cool then spread raspberry jam on whole cookies. Cover each with a cut-out cookie. Sprinkle each with powdered sugar.

Scotch Oven
Scones

2 C. flour
2 tsp. sugar
1/2 tsp. salt
1 tsp. cream of tartar

1 tsp. baking soda
1/2 C. margarine
3/4 C. milk

Preheat oven to 400°. In a medium bowl, sift together flour, sugar, salt, cream of tartar and baking soda. Cut in margarine until mixture is crumbly and crumbs are the size of peas. Pour in milk and mix with a fork until the crumb mixture is coated with liquid. The dough should be lumpy but hold together. Divide the dough in half. On a floured surface, shape dough into a circle, 1/2" thick. Cut dough into 4 or 6 wedges. Repeat with remaining dough. Bake for 10 to 12 minutes.

Lemony Butter Cookies

1/2 C. butter, softened
1/2 C. sugar
1 egg
1 1/2 C. flour
2 T. lemon juice

1 tsp. lemon zest
1/2 tsp. baking powder
1/8 tsp. salt
Additional sugar

In a large bowl, beat butter and sugar until creamy. Add egg and beat until light and fluffy. Stir in flour, lemon juice, zest, baking powder and salt. Cover and refrigerate for at least 2 hours or until firm. Preheat oven to 350°. On a floured surface, roll a small portion of the dough out at a time to 1/4" thickness. Cut into 3" circles and transfer to ungreased baking sheets. Sprinkle with additional sugar and bake for 8 to 10 minute or until edges are lightly browned.

Chocolate Pecan Crisps

1/2 C. butter or margarine,
    softened
1 C. packed brown sugar
1 egg
1 tsp. vanilla
1 1/2 C. flour

1 C. chopped pecans
1/3 C. unsweetened cocoa
    powder
1/2 tsp. baking soda
1 C. coconut

In a large bowl, cream butter and sugar until light and fluffy. Beat in egg and vanilla. In a separate bowl, mix flour, pecans, cocoa and baking soda. Add mixed dry ingredients to the creamed mixture and mix until a stiff dough is formed. Divide dough into 4 equal parts. Sprinkle coconut over work surface. Shape each dough piece into a roll that is approximately 1 1/2" in diameter. Roll in coconut until outside is well coated. Wrap each dough piece in plastic wrap and chill for at least 1 hour until firm. Preheat oven to 350°. Cut rolls into 1/8" thick slices. Place each cookie 2" apart on ungreased baking sheets. Bake for 10 to 13 minutes or until firm.

Coconut Butterballs

1 C. butter or margarine,
   softened
1/2 C. sugar
2 tsp. vanilla
2 C. flour

1/4 tsp. salt
2 C. pecan halves
1 egg white
1 T. water
3/4 to 1 C. coconut

Preheat oven to 350°. In a large bowl, cream butter, sugar and vanilla until fluffy. Blend in flour and salt and mix until thoroughly combined. Shape teaspoonfuls of dough around each pecan half to form a ball. Beat egg white and water with a fork until just frothy. Dip dough into egg white mixture and then into coconut, rolling until fully coated. Place balls onto a lightly greased baking sheet. Bake for 15 to 18 minutes or until lightly browned.

Date
Pinwheels

1 C. shortening
1 C. packed brown sugar
1/2 tsp. vanilla
1 egg
1 3/4 C. flour
1/2 tsp. baking soda

1/4 tsp. salt
3/4 C. chopped dates
1/3 C. sugar
1/3 C. water
1/2 C. chopped walnuts
    or pecans

In a medium bowl, cream shortening, brown sugar and vanilla until just fluffy. Stir in egg until combined. Add flour, baking soda and salt and beat on medium speed until well blended. For Date-Nut filling, combine chopped dates, sugar and water in a saucepan. Cook, stirring constantly, on medium heat until slightly thickened. Remove from heat and stir in nuts. Allow to cool. On a lightly floured surface, roll dough into 7 x 11" rectangles. Spread filling on each rectangle leaving a 1 1/2 to 2" border on 1 wide side of each. Beginning on wide side without the border, roll up in wax paper and chill for 2 to 3 hours. Preheat oven to 400°. Cut into 1/4" slices and place on a lightly greased baking sheet. Bake for 10 minutes.

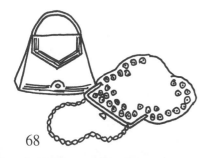

Chocolate-
Orange Biscotti

2 C. plus 2 T. flour
1 1/2 tsp. baking powder
3/4 C. sugar
1/2 C. butter, softened
2 eggs
2 T. Grand Marnier or
    other orange liqueur

1 T. orange zest
1 C. pecans, toasted*
    and chopped
6 oz. (3/4 C.) bittersweet
    chocolate, chopped

In a medium bowl, whisk together flour and baking powder. In a separate bowl, cream butter and sugar until light and fluffy. Beat in eggs, one at a time, then add in Grand Marnier and zest. Add flour mixture and beat until well blended. Stir in pecans and chocolate. Divide dough in half and wrap in plastic. Place in freezer for 20 minutes. Preheat oven to 350°. Using floured hands, form each dough piece into 14 x 2 1/2" logs. Transfer to a large baking sheet lined with parchment paper, spacing 2" apart. Bake for 30 minutes or until light golden. Transfer parchment paper and logs to a rack to cool for 20 minutes. Reduce oven temperature to 300°. Using a serrated knife cut 1/2" slices. Stand slices upright on baking sheet. Bake for an additional 30 minutes.

* To toast pecans, place nuts in a single layer on a baking sheet. Bake at 350° for approximately 10 minutes or until nuts are golden brown.

Sables

3/4 C. butter, softened
2/3 C. sugar
2 egg yolks
1 tsp. vanilla

2 C. cake flour
1 egg yolk
2 tsp. ice water

In a medium bowl, cream butter and sugar until fluffy. Add the 2 egg yolks and vanilla and stir until well blended. Add the flour in 2 parts, mixing until just combined before adding the second. Using wax paper, form the dough into two 3" diameter tubes. Wrap logs in plastic wrap and chill for 1 hour. Preheat oven to 350°. Cut dough into 1/8" disks and arrange on greased baking sheet. In a small bowl, lightly beat 1 egg yolk and ice water. Brush over each cookie. Bake for 8 to 10 minutes.

Cream Cheese Dainties

1 C. flour
1/2 C. butter or margarine,
  softened
4 oz. cream cheese, softened

1/3 C. fruit preserves
1 egg white
Sugar

In a medium bowl, cut butter and cream cheese into flour using a pastry blender until the mixture resembles fine crumbs. Knead dough against the sides of the bowl 5 to 10 times. Shape dough into a large ball and chill for 1 hour. Preheat oven to 375°. On a lightly floured surface, roll dough to approximately 1/16 to 1/8" thickness. Cut into 5 x 2 1/2" rectangles. Place 1 teaspoon of preserves in the center of each rectangle. Fold ends over middle and press together with a fork to seal. Brush tops with lightly beaten egg white and sprinkle each with a pinch of sugar. Bake for 15 minutes.

Brandy Snaps

1/2 C. butter
1/2 C. sugar
1/3 C. dark corn syrup
1/2 tsp. cinnamon

1/4 tsp. ginger
1 C. flour
2 tsp. brandy

Preheat oven to 300°. In a medium, heavy saucepan, combine butter, sugar, corn syrup, cinnamon and ginger over low heat, stirring until smooth. Remove from heat. Add flour and brandy and stir until well combined. Drop dough by rounded teaspoonfuls onto a ungreased baking sheet. Space each cookie 3" apart, baking no more than 6 at a time. Bake for 10 to 14 minutes or until a deep amber color. Immediately roll each cookie around a wooden spoon handle to shape.

Almond Thumbprint Cookies

1 1/2 C. flour
1/3 C. cornstarch
1/4 tsp. baking powder
1/4 tsp. baking soda
3 1/2 T. butter, softened
3 T. vegetable oil
1 T. light corn syrup

1/2 C. sugar
1 egg
1/4 tsp. lemon zest
2 1/2 tsp. vanilla
1/4 tsp. almond extract
Jam, flavor of your choice
Chopped almonds

Preheat oven to 375°. In a medium bowl, mix flour, cornstarch, baking powder and baking soda. In a separate bowl, beat butter, oil, corn syrup, sugar, egg, zest, vanilla and almond extract until well blended. Add dry ingredients and mix on low speed until just combined. Shape dough into 3/4" balls and place on a greased baking sheet. Make a deep thumbprint in the center of each cookie. Fill each well with jam. Lightly sprinkle each cookie with chopped almonds. Bake for 6 to 9 minutes or until slightly golden.

Melt Away Cookies

1 C. butter or margarine,
   softened
1/2 C. powdered sugar

1 tsp. vanilla
2 1/4 C. flour
1/4 tsp. salt

Preheat oven to 400°. In a large bowl, beat butter, sugar and vanilla on medium speed until well blended. Add flour and salt then mix until well combined. Drop by teaspoonfuls onto a greased baking sheet. Dough will not spread out like most cookies. Bake for 8 to 10 minutes or until set. Allow to cool slightly. While still warm, roll in powdered sugar.

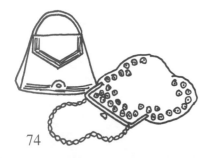

Chocolate Coconut Candies

3/4 C. mashed potatoes
   (homemade or instant)
4 C. coconut
4 1/2 C. powered sugar
1 tsp. almond extract

1/2 C. half and half
6 oz. semisweet or
    bittersweet chocolate
2 T. butter

In a large bowl, combine potatoes, coconut, powdered sugar and almond extract until well blended. Line baking sheet with wax paper. Shape into balls and place on baking sheet. Chill for 1 hour. In a double boiler, mix half and half, chocolate and butter and melt. Dip cooled coconut balls in chocolate coating then place on wax paper. Chill to set.

Apple Cinnamon Scones

1 1/2 C. flour
1/4 C. sugar
1 T. baking powder
1 1/4 C. oats
1 apple, peeled, cored
    and diced

1 egg
10 T. butter, melted
1/3 C. whole milk
Cinnamon Sugar

Preheat oven to 450°. In a large bowl, whisk together flour, sugar and baking powder. Stir in oats and diced apple. In a separate bowl, whisk together egg, butter and milk then add to dry ingredients until moistened. On a lightly floured surface, pat dough into an 8" circle about 3/4" thick. Cut into 8 to 12 wedges and place on a greased baking sheet. Sprinkle the tops with cinnamon sugar. Bake for 10 to 12 minutes.

Chocolate Pinwheels

3/4 C. shortening
1 C. sugar
2 eggs
2 1/2 C. flour
1 tsp. vanilla

1 tsp. baking powder
1 tsp. salt
2 oz. unsweetened
     chocolate, melted

In a large bowl, beat shortening and sugar on medium speed for 1 to 2 minutes until slightly fluffy. Blend in eggs and flour until well combined. Add vanilla, baking powder and salt and mix on medium speed until just combined. Split dough in half. To one half, add melted chocolate and blend until well combined. Chill both doughs for 1 hour. On a lightly floured surface, roll each dough into 9 x 12" rectangles. Lay one layer on top of the other then roll out dough again until thickness is approximately 1/4". Beginning at the wide side, roll dough together and chill for another hour. Preheat oven to 400°. Cut pinwheels into 1/8" slices and place on a greased baking sheet. Bake for 8 to 10 minutes.

Buttery Nut Rounds

1 C. butter or margarine,
   softened
1/2 C. powdered sugar
1 tsp. vanilla
2 1/4 C. flour

1/4 tsp. salt
3/4 C. finely chopped
   walnuts or pecans
Powdered sugar

In a large bowl, cream butter, sugar and vanilla until just fluffy. Blend in flour, salt and nuts until well combined. Chill dough for 1 hour. Preheat oven to 350°. On a lightly floured surface, roll dough out to 1/4" thickness. Cut into uniformly round cookies and place on a lightly greased baking sheet. Bake for 10 to 12 minutes. Allow cookies to cool completely. You can make tea cookie sandwiches by filling each with approximately a teaspoon full of fruit preserves, sweetened cream cheese, frosting, etc. Sprinkle tops with powdered sugar before serving.

Date Pecan Drop Scones

2 C. flour
1/4 C. sugar
4 tsp. baking powder
1/4 tsp. baking soda
1 egg

1 C. buttermilk
4 T. butter, melted
1/2 C. dates
1/3 C. finely chopped
    pecans

Preheat oven to 400°. In a large bowl, whisk together flour, sugar, baking powder and baking soda. In a separate bowl, mix egg, buttermilk, butter, dates and pecans then add to dry ingredients until moistened. Using a soup spoon, drop batter into 2 1/2" diameter mounds onto a greased baking sheet. Bake for 12 to 15 minutes or until tops are lightly browned.

Coconut Macaroons

2/3 C. sweetened
   condensed milk
1 egg white

1 1/2 tsp. vanilla
1/8 tsp. salt
3 1/2 C. coconut

Preheat oven to 325°. In a medium bowl, combine sweetened condensed milk, egg white, vanilla and salt. Stir until well blended. Stir in coconut. Line a baking sheet with parchment or wax paper. Drop tablespoonfuls of dough onto baking sheet. Bake for 20 to 25 minutes or until lightly browned.

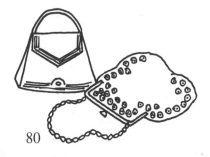

Desserts

Peanut Butter Chocolate Truffles

1 C. peanut butter baking
   chips
3/4 C. margarine
1/2 C. unsweetened cocoa powder
1 (14 oz.) can sweetened
   condensed milk

1 T. vanilla
Finely chopped nuts,
   graham cracker crumbs,
   powdered sugar or
   unsweetened cocoa
   powder

In a heavy saucepan, over low heat, melt peanut butter chips and margarine. Stir in cocoa until mixture is smooth. Add condensed milk and vanilla. Cook, stirring constantly, for approximately 4 minutes, until thickened and well blended. Remove from heat and chill for 2 hours or until firm enough to shape. Shape mixture into 1" balls and roll in nuts, graham cracker crumbs, powdered sugar or cocoa. Chill for approximately 1 hour or until firm. Store, covered, in refrigerator. Serve at room temperature for the best flavor.

Layered Angel Food Cake

1 angel food cake mix
1 (20 oz.) can crushed
  pineapple, undrained
1 (3 oz.) pkg. cook & serve
  pudding mix

2 C. (1 pint) whipping cream
1/3 C. chopped maraschino
  cherries

Bake angel food cake according to package directions and cool completely. In a heavy saucepan, mix the pineapple and pudding mix then cook over medium heat, stirring constantly, until mixture is very thick. Remove from heat. Cool and refrigerate until well chilled. Cut the angel food cake horizontally into three layers. Whip the cream and fold into pineapple mixture then add the chopped maraschino cherries. Spread mixture generously between the layers and over the top of the cake. Refrigerate cake until ready to serve.

Lemon Tea Bars

1 C. flour	2 T. flour
1/4 C. powdered sugar	1 T. lemon zest
1/2 C. butter, softened	1/2 tsp. baking powder
2 eggs	2 T. lemon juice
1 C. sugar	Powdered sugar

Preheat the oven to 350°. In a large bowl, combine 1 cup flour and 1/4 cup powdered sugar. Using a pastry blender, two knives or a wire whisk, cut in butter until mixture resembles coarse crumbs. Press the crumb mixture into the bottom of a lightly greased 8 or 9" square pan. Bake for 15 minutes. Meanwhile, in a small bowl, combine eggs and sugar until well mixed. Stir in 2 tablespoons flour, lemon zest, baking powder and lemon juice. Pour filling over the partially baked crust. Return to the oven and bake for 18 to 25 minutes or until light golden brown. Cool completely. If desired, sift additional powdered sugar over the bars.

Petite Cherry Tarts

2 (8 oz.) pkgs. cream
    cheese, softened
2 eggs
1/2 C. sugar
1 T. lemon juice

1 tsp. vanilla
1 (21 oz.) can cherry
    pie filling
Vanilla wafers

Preheat oven to 350°. In a medium bowl, mix cream cheese, eggs, sugar, lemon juice and vanilla with a fork until blended then beat until well combined. Line muffin tins with papers. Place a vanilla wafer in the bottom of each paper and fill half full with cream cheese mixture. Bake for 15 minutes. Cool completely before topping each tart with a cherry pie filling. Chill in refrigerator.

Fudge Mint Petits Fours

4 oz. unsweetened chocolate
1 1/2 C. sugar, divided
6 T. water
1/2 C. shortening
1 tsp. vanilla
3 eggs
2 C. flour
1 tsp. baking soda

1/4 tsp. salt
2/3 C. milk
1 C. powdered sugar
1/2 C. butter, partially melted
2 T. crème de menthe liqueur
1 C. chocolate chips
6 T. butter

Preheat oven to 350°. In a heavy saucepan or double boiler over low heat, combine unsweetened chocolate, 1/2 cup sugar and water. Mix until melted, stirring constantly, and set aside. In a medium bowl, cream together shortening and remaining 1 cup sugar, until lightened in texture. Stir in vanilla and eggs and beat until thoroughly combined. In a separate bowl, combine flour, baking soda and salt. Alternating, pour flour mixture and milk, in 3 parts, into eggs mixture. Mix well and pour in melted chocolate mixture, stirring until well blended. Pour batter into a greased 9 x 13" pan and bake for 35 to 40 minutes. Cool cake completely. In a small bowl, combine powdered sugar, 1/2 cup partially melted butter and crème de menthe, until well blended. Spread mixture over cooled cake. In a small saucepan, melt chocolate chips and 6 tablespoons butter. Let cool slightly before spreading over green layer. Chill cake and cut into squares. Refrigerate. Can be frozen.

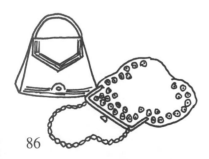

Chocolate Truffle Cake

2/3 C. butter
1 (12 oz.) pkg. chocolate
    chips
1 1/2 tsp. flour

1 1/2 tsp. sugar
1/2 tsp. salt
4 eggs, separated
Whipped topping

Preheat oven to 325°. Melt butter and chocolate chips in top of a double broiler. Add flour, sugar and salt and stir until well combined. Beat in egg yolks one at a time. In a separate bowl, beat egg whites until stiff then fold into chocolate mixture. Pour into a greased and floured deep, 8" inch cake or spring form pan. Bake for approximately 40 minutes or until a toothpick inserted in the center comes out clean. Cool for 15 minutes before cutting. Top with whipped topping.

Chocolate Raspberry Truffle Cheesecake

1 1/2 C. finely crushed graham
   crackers or chocolate crème
   filled cookie crumbs
2 T. margarine, melted
4 (8 oz.) pkgs. cream cheese,
   softened, divided
1 1/4 C. sugar
3 eggs

1 C. sour cream
1 tsp. vanilla
1 C. semisweet chocolate
   chips, divided
1/2 C. seedless raspberry
   preserves
1/4 C. whipping cream
Whipped cream, optional

Preheat oven to 325°. Combine crumbs and margarine to form crust mixture. Press into the bottom of a 9" spring form pan. Set aside. In a large mixing bowl, combine 3 packages of the cream cheese and sugar. Mix on medium speed until well blended. Add eggs, one at a time, and mix well. Blend in the sour cream and vanilla. Pour mixture over the crust and set aside. Melt 1/2 cup chocolate chips then combine with remaining package of cream cheese. Add preserves and mix well. Drop chocolate raspberry mixture by rounded tablespoonsful over the plain batter but do not swirl. Bake for 1 hour and 20 minutes or until center is almost set. Loosen pan rim and set aside to cool. For topping, warm whipping cream over low heat and add remaining 1/2 cup chocolate chips. Mix well and spread over cheesecake. Chill. Serve with whipped cream, if desired.

Blueberry Cheesecake

1 1/4 C. crushed vanilla
    wafers
2 T. sugar
3 T. butter or margarine,
    melted
3 (8 oz.) pkgs. cream
    cheese, softened
1 C. sugar

2 tsp. lemon zest
1 tsp. vanilla
3 eggs
1 C. fresh or frozen
    blueberries
1/2 C. sugar
2 T. cornstarch
1 C. water

Preheat oven to 300°. Combine wafer crumbs, 2 tablespoons sugar and butter. Press into the bottom of a 9" spring form pan. In a large bowl, beat cream cheese, gradually adding sugar. Continue to beat until fluffy. Add lemon rind and vanilla. Beat in eggs, one at a time. Pour over crust. Bake for 1 hour or until center is firm. Cool to room temperature. Meanwhile, in a small saucepan, stir together 1/2 cup sugar, cornstarch and water. Add blueberries. Cook and stir until mixture thickens. Cool. Spread on cheesecake and refrigerate several hours before serving.

Turtle
Cheesecake

1/2 C. flour
1/4 C. packed brown sugar
1/4 C. butter or margarine,
   softened
4 (8 oz.) pkgs. cream
   cheese, softened
1 1/4 C. packed brown sugar

4 eggs
1 C. heavy cream
1 C. whipped cream
3/4 C. caramel flavored ice
   cream topping
1 C. crushed pecans

Preheat oven to 350°. Mix flour, 1/4 cup brown sugar and butter with pastry blender, two forks or a wire whisk. Press mixture into the bottom and up sides of a 9" spring form pan. Bake for 8 minutes. Set aside. Reduce oven temperature to 300°. In a large mixing bowl, blend cream cheese, sugar, eggs and heavy cream. Beat well and pour into prepared crust. Bake for 1 hour and 15 minutes or until almost set. Cool. Release pan rim and refrigerate for 8 hours. Spread with whipped and carefully swirl in caramel ice cream topping. Top with pecans.

Tiny Pecan Tarts

1/2 C. butter, softened
1 (3 oz.) pkg. cream
    cheese, softened
1 C. flour
1 egg

3/4 C. packed brown
    sugar
1 T. margarine, melted
1/2 C. chopped pecans

Preheat oven to 325°. In a medium bowl, beat butter and cream cheese until thoroughly blended then stir in flour. Place a rounded teaspoonful into 24 ungreased mini muffin cups. Press dough evenly into the bottom and up the sides of each cup. In another bowl, beat egg and mix in brown sugar, margarine and chopped pecans. Fill each pastry lined muffin cup with 1 heaping tablespoon of pecan filling. Bake for 30 minutes or until pastry is golden and filling is puffed. Cool slightly in the muffin cups, then remove and cool completely on a wire rack.

Black Forest
Mini Cheesecakes

24 vanilla wafers
2 (8 oz.) pkgs. cream
    cheese, softened
1 1/4 C. sugar
1/3 C. unsweetened
    cocoa powder
2 T. flour
3 eggs

1 C. sour cream
1/2 tsp. almond extract
1 C. sour cream
2 T. sugar
1 tsp. vanilla
1 (21 oz.) can cherry pie
    filling, chilled

Preheat oven to 325°. Line regular sized muffin cups with foil muffin papers. Place 1 vanilla wafer in the bottom of each cup. In a large bowl, beat cream cheese until smooth. Add 1 1/4 cup sugar, cocoa and flour and mix until well blended. Add eggs and beat well. Stir in 1 cup sour cream and almond extract. Fill each muffin cup 3/4 full with batter. In a separate bowl, mix together 1 cup sour cream, 2 tablespoons sugar and 1 teaspoon vanilla. Bake for 20 to 25 minutes or until set. Remove from oven and cool for 5 to 10 minutes. Spread a heaping teaspoon of the sour cream mixture over each cheesecake. Cool completely in pan then refrigerate. Just before serving, garnish with cherry pie filling.

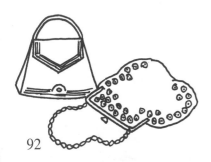

Graham Streusel Coffee Cake

1 1/3 C. graham cracker
   crumbs
3/4 C. chopped walnuts
3/4 C. packed brown
   sugar
1 1/2 tsp. cinnamon
2/3 C. butter, melted

1 (18.25 oz.) pkg.
   yellow cake mix
1 C. water
1/4 C. vegetable oil
3 eggs
1 C. powdered sugar
1 1/2 tsp. vanilla
Water

Preheat oven to 350°. In a medium bowl, combine the graham cracker crumbs, walnuts, brown sugar and cinnamon. Stir in the melted butter until well combined. Set aside. In a large mixing bowl, combine the cake mix, water, oil and eggs. Beat on low speed until just moistened. Beat on medium speed for an additional 2 minutes. Spread half of the batter into a greased 9 x 13" pan. Sprinkle on half of the streusel mixture. Carefully spread the remaining cake batter over the streusel and sprinkle cake with the remaining streusel. Bake for 35 to 40 minutes or until a toothpick inserted in the center comes out clean. In a small bowl, mix powder sugar and vanilla. Add a few drops of water until you achieve drizzling consistency. Drizzle icing over slightly cooled cake.

Sour Cream Coffee Cake

1/3 C. flour
1/2 C. packed brown sugar
2 T. melted butter
1 tsp. cinnamon
1 C. butter
2 C. sugar

2 eggs
1 C. sour cream
1/2 tsp. vanilla
2 C. flour
1 tsp. baking powder
1/8 tsp. salt

Preheat the oven to 350°. In a medium bowl, mix 1/3 cup flour, brown sugar, 2 tablespoons melted butter and cinnamon. Set aside. In a large bowl, cream together 1 cup butter and sugar until light and fluffy. Beat in eggs one at a time then stir in sour cream and vanilla. Mix in 2 cups flour, baking powder and salt. Spread half of the batter into a greased 9 x 13" pan then sprinkle half of the filling over batter. Carefully spread remaining batter over the filling then top with the remaining filling. Bake for 35 to 40 minutes or until a toothpick inserted in the center comes out clean.

Southern Praline Pecan Cake

1 (18.25 oz.) pkg. Betty
    Crocker butter
    pecan cake mix
1 (16 oz.) container coconut
    pecan frosting

4 eggs
2/3 C. vegetable oil
3/4 C. water
1 C. chopped pecans,
    divided

Preheat oven to 350°. In a large bowl, combine the cake mix, frosting, eggs, oil, water and 1/2 cup chopped pecans. Mix until well combined. Grease a 9 or 10" Bundt pan then sprinkle the remaining pecan pieces into the prepared pan. Pour cake batter over sprinkles in pan. Bake for 50 minutes or until a toothpick inserted in the center comes out clean.

Apricot Danish Coffee Cake

1 (18.25 oz.) pkg. white
    cake mix
3 eggs
1 1/2 C. sour cream
1 (15 oz.) can apricot
    halves, drained
1 T. butter, softened

1/2 C. slivered almonds
1 (8 oz.) pkg. cream
    cheese, softened
2 T. milk
2/3 C. powdered sugar
2 tsp. water

Preheat oven to 350°. Set aside a 1/2 cup of the cake mix. In a medium bowl, mix together eggs and sour cream. Stir in the remaining cake mix. Batter will be lumpy. Spread into a greased and floured 10 x 15" jellyroll pan. Using the back of a wooden spoon, make 15 wells in the batter (3 rows of 5). In another bowl, beat together cream cheese and milk until fluffy. Place 1 tablespoon of the cream cheese mixture into each well then place 1 apricot half, cut side up, over the cream cheese. In a small bowl, combine the 1/2 cup of reserved cake mix and butter until crumbly. Stir in the almonds and sprinkle mixture evenly over the cake. Bake for 30 to 35 minutes or until a toothpick inserted in the center of the cake comes out clean. In another small bowl, mix powdered sugar and water until smooth. Drizzle icing over cooled cake.

Pecan Pie Squares

1 C. flour
1/2 C. packed brown sugar
1/2 C. butter
2 eggs
1/2 C. light corn syrup

1/2 C. packed brown sugar
2 T. butter, melted
1 tsp. vanilla
1/4 tsp. salt
3/4 C. chopped pecans

Preheat oven to 350°. In a medium bowl, mix flour and 1/2 cup brown sugar. Cut butter in with your hands until the mixture is blended enough to form a ball. Press the dough evenly into a greased and floured 9 x 9" pan. Bake for 5 to 7 minutes. In another medium bowl, beat the eggs then add corn syrup, 1/2 cup brown sugar, butter, vanilla and salt. Mix until well blended. Stir in chopped pecans. Pour over the semi-baked dough. Bake for 30 minutes. To serve, cut into small squares as they are very rich.

Butterscotch Bars

1 C. butter, softened
1/2 C. sugar
1/2 C. packed brown sugar
2 egg yolks
1 T. milk

1 tsp. vanilla
2 C. flour, sifted
1 tsp. baking powder
1 tsp. salt
1 C. butterscotch chips

Preheat the oven to 350°. In a large bowl, cream the butter, sugar and brown sugar. Add the egg yolks, milk and vanilla and mix until well blended. In a separate bowl, mix flour, baking powder and salt. Stir into the creamed mixture until well blended. Stir in butterscotch chips. Spread dough evenly into a greased and floured 9 x 13" pan. Bake for 25 to 30 minutes or until the top is lightly browned.

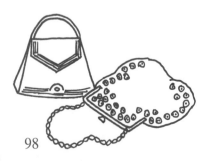

Rum
Truffles

6 (1 oz.) unsweetened
   chocolate squares
2 T. butter
1 T. heavy cream
6 T. dark rum

2 egg yolks
2 C. powdered sugar,
   sifted
Unsweetened cocoa
   powder

In a heavy saucepan, melt the chocolate and butter over low heat, stirring constantly. Remove from heat and add the cream and rum and blend well. Stir in the egg yolks and powdered sugar. Knead dough with your hands until the mixture is smooth. Refrigerate for 30 minutes. Shape dough into 1" balls. Roll each ball in cocoa. Refrigerate for at least 30 minutes before serving.

Strawberry Crumb Bars

1 1/4 C. flour
1/3 C. packed brown sugar
1/2 C. butter, softened
3/4 C. strawberry preserves

1/2 C. flour
1/2 C. packed brown sugar
1/4 C. butter, softened
1/2 tsp. almond extract

Preheat oven to 350°. In a small bowl, combine 1 1/4 cup flour, 1/3 cup brown sugar and 1/2 cup butter. Mix until mixture is crumbly. Press into a greased and floured 8 or 9" inch square pan. Bake for 15 to 20 minutes or until edges are lightly browned. Spread preserves to within 1/4" of the edge. In a small bowl, combine 1/2 cup flour, 1/2 cup brown sugar, 1/4 cup butter and 1/2 teaspoon almond extract. Mix until well blended. Sprinkle topping over preserves. Bake for 20 to 25 minutes or until edges are lightly browned.

Lemon Poppy Seed Pound Cake

3 C. flour
2 C. sugar
1/4 C. poppy seeds
1 C. butter, softened
1 C. buttermilk
4 eggs
1/2 tsp. baking soda

1/2 tsp. baking powder
1/2 tsp. salt
4 tsp. lemon zest
1/2 tsp. vanilla
1 C. powdered sugar
1 - 2 T. lemon juice

Preheat oven to 325°. In a large bowl, mix flour, sugar, poppy seeds, butter, buttermilk, eggs, baking soda, baking powder, salt, zest and vanilla until well combined. Pour batter into a greased and floured Bundt pan. Bake for 55 to 65 minutes or until a toothpick inserted into the center comes out clean. Cool for 10 minutes then remove from pan. In a small bowl, mix powdered sugar and lemon juice until smooth. Drizzle over cooled cake.

Raspberry Oatmeal Bars

1 (18.25 oz.) pkg. yellow cake mix
2 1/2 C. quick oats
3/4 C. butter or margarine, melted

1 C. raspberry preserves
1 T. water

Preheat oven to 375°. In a large bowl, combine dry cake mix and oats. Add butter and mix until crumbly. Place half of the crumb mixture into a greased 9 x 13" pan. Press firmly over bottom to make a crust. Combine preserves and water and spread evenly over crust. Sprinkle remaining crumb mixture over preserves and pat lightly. Bake for 18 to 23 minutes or until top is very light brown.

Blueberry
Angel Cake Rolls

1 pkg. angel food cake mix	1 (21 oz.) can blueberry
Powdered sugar	pie filling

Preheat oven to 350°. Prepare cake batter according to package directions. Line two 10 x 15" jellyroll pans with foil. Divide batter between pans and spread evenly being sure to remove large air bubbles. Bake for 15 minutes or until a toothpick inserted in the center comes out clean. Invert cakes at once onto clean dishtowels dusted with powdered sugar. Carefully remove the foil. Starting at short end, roll up each cake with towel. Cool completely. Unroll cakes and spread each with half of the blueberry pie filling to within 1" of the edges. Reroll and place seam side down on a serving plate. Slice and serve.

Ribbon Carrot Cake

1 (8 oz.) pkg. cream cheese,
   softened
1/4 C. sugar
1 egg, beaten
2 C. flour
1 3/4 C. sugar
2 tsp. baking soda

2 tsp. cinnamon
1 tsp. salt
1 C. oil
3 eggs, beaten
3 C. shredded carrot
1/2 C. chopped nuts
Powdered sugar

Preheat oven to 350°. In a small bowl, mix cream cheese, 1/4 cup sugar and egg until well blended. Set aside. In a large bowl, combine flour, 1 3/4 cup sugar, baking soda, cinnamon and salt. Mix oil and eggs together then add to dry ingredients and stir until just moistened. Fold in shredded carrots and nuts. Reserve 2 cups batter and pour the rest into a greased and floured 9" Bundt pan. Pour cream cheese mixture over the batter and then carefully spoon reserved batter over the cream cheese layer, spreading to completely cover. Bake for 55 minutes or until a toothpick inserted in the center comes out clean. Cool for 10 minutes before removing from pan. Cool completely then sprinkle with powdered sugar, if desired.

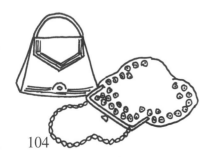

Lemon Cheesecake

2 (8 oz.) pkgs. cream cheese,
   softened
1/2 C. sugar
1 T. fresh lemon juice
1/2 tsp. lemon zest

1/2 tsp. vanilla
2 eggs
1 -9" graham cracker
   crumb crust
Whipped cream, optional

Preheat oven to 350°. In a medium bowl, mix cream cheese, sugar, lemon juice, zest and vanilla. Beat on medium speed until smooth. Add eggs and mix until well blended. Pour mixture into graham cracker crumb crust. Bake for 40 minutes or until center is almost set. Refrigerate for at least 3 hours before serving. Garnish with whipped cream, if desired.

Viennese Torte

1 (6 oz.) pkg. semisweet
  chocolate chips
1/2 C. butter or margarine
1/4 C. water
4 egg yolks, slightly beaten

1/4 C. powdered sugar
1 tsp. vanilla
1 (12 oz.) loaf frozen pound
  cake, thawed

In a heavy saucepan, heat butter and water. Add chocolate chips and melt over medium heat until smooth, stirring constantly. Cool slightly then pour into a small mixing bowl. Gradually add egg yolks, powdered sugar and vanilla. Blend until smooth. Chill for approximately 45 minutes until mixture is of a spreading consistency. Beat until thick. Slice cake horizontally until you get 5 layers. Frost between each layer with chocolate mixture then frost top and sides. Chill for at least another 45 minutes before slicing thin to serve.

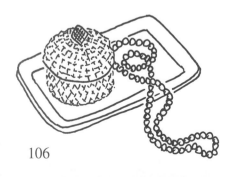

Brownie Bottom
Cheesecake

1 (10 to 20 oz.) pkg.
   brownie mix
3 (8 oz.) pkgs. cream
   cheese, softened

3/4 C. sugar
1 tsp. vanilla
1/2 C. sour cream
3 eggs

Prepare brownie mix according to package instructions for a 9" square pan or a well-greased 9" spring form pan. Cool. Preheat oven to 325°. In a large bowl, mix cream cheese, sugar and vanilla. Beat on medium speed until well blended. Stir in sour cream. Add eggs and mix on low speed just until blended. Pour mixture over brownie crust. Bake for 1 hour to 1 hour and 5 minutes or until center is almost set. Loosen cheesecake by running a knife along the sides of the pan. Cool before removing cake. Refrigerate for at least 4 hours before serving.

Strawberries 'n Cream Tart

1/2 C. butter, softened
1/3 C. sugar
1 1/4 C. flour
2 T. milk
1/2 tsp. almond extract
1 (3 oz.) pkg. cream cheese,
   softened

1/2 C. powdered sugar
1/2 tsp. almond extract
1 C. whipping cream
1 pint fresh strawberries,
   sliced
2 - 4 T. strawberry jelly,
   melted

Preheat oven to 400°. In a small bowl, beat butter and sugar until light and fluffy. Add flour, milk and 1/2 teaspoon almond extract. Continue beating until mixture forms a ball then press dough on bottom and up sides of a greased 10" tart pan or a 12" pizza pan. Prick entire dough surface with a fork. Bake for 10 to 15 minutes or until crust is a light golden brown. Cool. In a small bowl, beat cream cheese, powdered sugar and 1/2 teaspoon almond extract until light and fluffy. Gradually add whipping cream and continue to beat until mixture is thick and fluffy. Spread mixture over the cooled crust. Chill for at least 1 hour. Just before serving arrange strawberries over filling then brush with melted jelly.

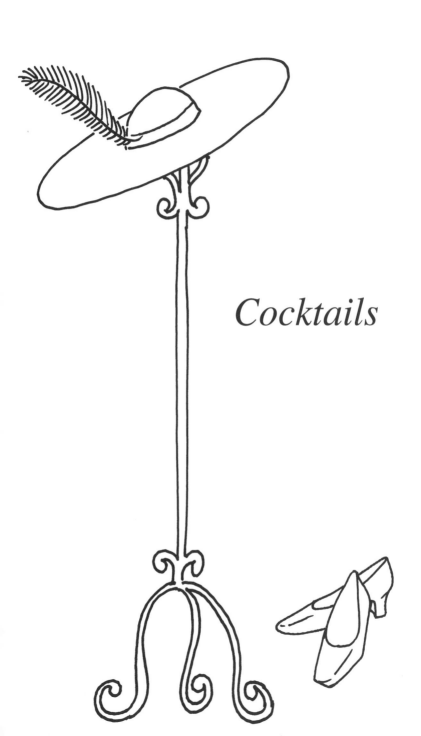

Cocktails

Southern Sunshine

2 C. orange juice
1/2 C. lemon juice
1/4 C. sugar

1 (32 oz.) bottle lemon-lime
   soda, chilled
3/4 C. Southern Comfort
Ice

In a pitcher, combine orange juice, lemon juice and sugar. Stir until sugar is dissolved. Cover and chill. Just before serving add soda and Southern Comfort. Serve over ice.

Bloody Mary

3 C. tomato juice, chilled
3/4 C. vodka
4 tsp. lemon juice
2 tsp. Worcestershire sauce

1/2 tsp. celery salt
1/8 tsp. Tabasco sauce
Dash pepper

In a pitcher, combine tomato juice, vodka, lemon juice, Worcestershire sauce, celery salt, Tabasco sauce and pepper until well mixed. Serve over ice.

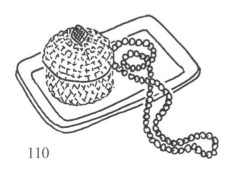

Mai Tai Slush

1 1/2 C. pineapple juice
1 pint (2 C.) lemon or
  lime sherbet

1 C. crushed ice
1/4 C. rum
2 T. orange liqueur

In a blender, combine pineapple juice, sherbet, crushed ice, rum and orange liqueur. Blend until well mixed. Pour into glasses to serve.

Sangria

3/4 C. sugar
3/4 C. orange juice
1/3 C. lemon juice
1/3 C. lime juice

2 (750 ml.) bottles medium-
  dry red wine, chilled
Ice

In a pitcher, combine sugar, orange juice, lemon juice and lime juice. Stir until sugar dissolves. Cover and chill. Just before serving, add wine. Serve over ice.

Champagne Punch

3 C. pineapple juice, chilled
1/4 C. lemon juice

1 qt. pineapple sherbet
1 (750 ml.) bottle champagne,
    chilled

In a punch bowl, combine pineapple juice and lemon juice. Scoop sherbet into punch bowl and pour champagne over all. Stir carefully to mix. Serve immediately.

Purple Passion

1 (6 oz.) can grape juice
    concentrate, thawed
3 juice cans cold water
1 juice can vodka

1/2 C. lemon juice
1/4 C. sugar
Ice

In a pitcher, combine grape juice concentrate, water, vodka, lemon juice and sugar. Stir until sugar dissolves. Cover and chill. Serve over ice.

Bourbon Slush

2 C. brewed tea
1 (6 oz.) can orange juice
    concentrate, thawed
1/3 C. sugar

2 C. cold water
1 C. bourbon
1/3 C. lemon juice

In a large bowl, combine tea, orange juice concentrate and sugar. Stir until sugar is dissolved. Add water, bourbon and lemon juice and mix well. Cover and freeze for at least 1 hour. Remove from freezer and thaw until mixture is slushy. Spoon into cocktail glasses and serve.

Lemony Light Cooler

1 (750 ml.) bottle dry white
    wine, chilled
1/2 C. sugar

1/2 C. lemon juice
1 (32 oz.) bottle club soda, chilled
Ice

In a pitcher, combine wine, sugar and lemon juice. Stir until sugar is dissolved. Cover and chill. Just before serving add club soda. Serve over ice.

Sangria Blush

1 C. orange juice
1/2 C. sugar
1 (1.5 liter) bottle white
   Zinfandel wine

1/4 C. lime or lemon juice
1 orange, thinly sliced
1 lime, thinly sliced
20 ice cubes

In a small pan, combine orange juice and sugar. Cook over medium heat, stirring occasionally, until sugar is dissolved. Pour into a 2-quart container. Add wine, lime or lemon juice, orange slices and lime slices. Cover tightly and refrigerate for at least 2 hours. Place ice cubes in a pitcher and pour wine mixture over ice.

Frozen Margaritas

1/2 C. tequila
1/3 C. lime juice
1/4 C. triple sec

1 C. powdered sugar
4 C. ice cubes

In a blender, combine tequila, lime juice, triple sec and powdered sugar. Blend well. Gradually add ice until smooth. Pour into glasses to serve.

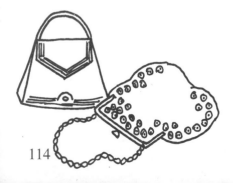

Strawberry
Frozen Margaritas

1 (10 oz.) pkg. frozen strawberries,
    partially thawed
1/4 C. lime juice
1/4 C. tequila

2 T. triple sec
1/4 C. powdered sugar
3 C. ice cubes

In a blender, combine strawberries, lime juice, tequila, triple sec and powdered sugar. Blend well. Gradually add ice until smooth. Pour into glasses to serve.

Party Mai Tais

3 C. pineapple juice, chilled
1 C. light rum
1 (6 oz.) can orange juice
    concentrate, thawed

1/2 C. lemon juice
Ice

In a pitcher, combine pineapple juice, rum, orange juice and lemon juice. Stir until well combined. Serve over ice.

Brandy Slush

7 C. water
1 (12 oz.) can lemonade
    concentrate, thawed
1 (12 oz.) can orange juice
    concentrate, thawed

1 1/2 C. sugar
2 C. brandy, any flavor
Lemon-lime soda

In a large bowl, combine water, lemonade, orange juice and sugar. Stir until sugar is dissolved. Stir in brandy. Cover and freeze for at least 1 hour. Remove from freezer and thaw until mixture is slushy. To serve, mix equal amounts of slush and lemon-lime soda.

Piña Colada

2 C. pineapple juice, chilled
1 1/2 C. rum

1 C. canned cream of coconut
8 C. crushed ice

In a blender, combine pineapple juice, rum, cream of coconut and crushed ice. Blend well. Pour into glasses to serve.

Spiked Fruit Slush

1 (12 oz.) can lemonade
   concentrate, thawed
1 (12 oz.) can fruit punch
   concentrate, thawed
7 C. water
1 1/2 C. sugar

2 C. hot water with 2 tea
   bags added
1 C. watermelon schnapps
1 C. vodka
1/4 C. sloe gin
Lemon-lime soda

In a large bowl, combine lemonade, fruit punch, water, sugar, hot water with tea, watermelon schnapps, vodka and sloe gin. Stir until sugar is dissolved. Cover and freeze. Stir once every 8 to 10 hours. Remove from freezer and thaw until mixture is slushy. To serve, mix equal amounts of slush and lemon-lime soda.

Shirley Temple

3/4 C. lemon-lime soda
1 dash grenadine syrup

1 maraschino cherry
Ice

In a tall glass, pour soda over ice. Add a dash of grenadine syrup and stir until well mixed. Top with a maraschino cherry.

Bikini Martini

2 T. coconut rum
1 1/2 T. vodka
2 T. pineapple juice

1 dash grenadine syrup
Orange, sliced

Combine rum, vodka and pineapple juice in a drink shaker. Shake firmly until frothy. Pour into a martini glass and add a dash of grenadine syrup in the center. Garnish with an orange wheel.

Frozen Mudslide

8 C. crushed ice
3/4 C. vodka
3/4 C. coffee flavored liqueur

3/4 C. Irish cream liqueur
1 C. whipped cream

In a blender, combine crushed ice, vodka, coffee liqueur and Irish cream liqueur. Drizzle chocolate syrup over all. Blend until smooth. Pour into glasses and top with whipped cream.

Crème de Menthe Punch

1 C. sugar
1/2 C. water
1/2 C. grapefruit juice
Juice of 6 oranges
Juice of 6 lemons

1/2 C. crème de menthe
1/4 C. crushed pineapple
Rind of 1 cucumber
1 liter lemon-lime soda

In a small saucepan, heat sugar and water and stir. Cool then add grapefruit juice, orange juice, lemon juice, crème de menthe, pineapple and cucumber rind to the water and sugar mixture. Chill for at least 2 hours. Just before serving, remove cucumber rind and add lemon-lime soda.

Hot Buttered Rum

1 C. sugar	Rum
1 C. packed brown sugar	Boiling water
1 C. butter	Ground nutmeg
2 C. vanilla ice cream, softened	

In a large saucepan, combine sugar, brown sugar and butter. Cook, stirring occasionally, over low heat until butter melts and sugar is dissolved, approximately 6 to 8 minutes. Transfer mixture to a large bowl and add ice cream. Beat on medium speed until completely smooth. Store in refrigerator for up to 2 weeks before serving. To serve, fill each mug with 1/4 cup mixture, 1 ounce rum and 3/4 cup boiling water then sprinkle with nutmeg.

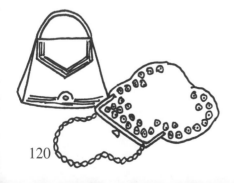

Index

Finger Sandwiches

Almond Chicken Salad 17
Apricot Ham Finger Sandwiches 21
Bacon & Egg Sandwiches 4
Beef and Cheddar Rolls 22
Celery-Nut Sandwiches 19
Chicken & Pineapple Sandwiches 12
Crab Salad Sandwiches 8
Cranberry Fingers 18
Crunchy Chicken Salad Sandwiches 5
Cucumber Sandwiches 14
Cucumber Tea Sandwiches 11
Egg Salad Sandwiches 15
Fancy Tuna Salad Sandwiches 6
Pineapple Cream Sandwiches 20
Pineapple Nut Sandwiches 10
Parsley, Olive & Tuna Salad Rolls 23
Olive Pecan Cream Sandwiches 24
Simple, Elegant Chicken Salad Sandwiches 3
Smoked Salmon Sandwiches 16
Strawberry Delight Sandwiches 9
Turkey Havarti Rolls 7
Turkey Orange Sandwiches 22
Typical tea sandwich shapes 2
Walnut Tuna Sandwiches 13

Pastries

Apple Pastry 35
Apricot Shortcakes 36
Chocolate Croissants 29
Cream Puffs 32
Danish Puff 26
Fruit Crostata 30

Fruit Turnovers 37
Gobbet Cakes 38
Kolachky 27
Lemon Curd Tartlets 34
Peach Tart Tatin 28
Scottish Shortbread 31
White Chocolate Cranberry Pear Pastry 33

Cookies & Scones

Almond Thumbprint Cookies 73
Apple Cinnamon Scones 76
Biscotti Toscani 56
Brandy Snaps 72
Brownie Biscotti 46
Butter Pecan Rounds 51
Buttery Nut Rounds 78
Chocolate Chip Scones 49
Chocolate Coconut Candies 75
Chocolate Linzer Cookies 60
Chocolate-Orange Biscotti 69
Chocolate Pecan Crisps 66
Chocolate Pinwheels 77
Cinnamon Drops 60
Cinnamon Hazelnut Biscotti 45
Coffee House Scones 48
Coconut Butterballs 67
Coconut Macaroons 80
Cranberry Drops 43
Cream Cheese Cookies 44
Cream Cheese Dainties 71
Cream Scones 42
Danish Oatmeal Cookies 40
Date Pecan Drop Scones 79
Date Pinwheels 68
Gingersnap Cookies 41
Iced Molasses Cookies 62
Lemony Butter Cookies 65
Lemon Chewy Crisps 58
Lemon Sugar Tea Cookies 47
Linzer Cookies 63
Melt Away Cookies 74
Oatmeal Raisin Cookies 52

Oatmeal Toffee Cookies 53
Orange Almond Biscotti 59
Pecan Filled Cookies 54
Raspberry and Almond Shortbread Thumbprints 57
Sables 70
Scotch Oven Scones 64
Shortbread Chocolate Chip Cookies 55
Walnut Raisin Scones 50

Desserts

Apricot Danish Coffee Cake 96
Black Forest Mini Cheesecakes 92
Blueberry Angel Cake Rolls 103
Blueberry Cheesecake 89
Brownie Bottom Cheesecake 107
Butterscotch Bars 98
Chocolate Raspberry Truffle Cheesecake 88
Chocolate Truffle Cake 87
Fudge Mint Petits Fours 86
Graham Streusel Coffee Cake 93
Layered Angel Food Cake 83
Lemon Cheesecake 105
Lemon Poppy Seed Pound Cake 101
Lemon Tea Bars 84
Peanut Butter Chocolate Truffles 82
Pecan Pie Squares 97
Petite Cherry Tarts 85
Raspberry Oatmeal Bars 102
Ribbon Carrot Cake 104
Rum Truffles 99
Sour Cream Coffee Cake 94
Southern Praline Pecan Cake 95
Strawberries 'n Cream Tart 108
Strawberry Crumb Bars 100
Tiny Pecan Tarts 91
Turtle Cheesecake 90
Viennese Torte 106

Cocktails

Bikini Martini 118
Bloody Mary 110

Bourbon Slush 113
Brandy Slush 116
Champagne Punch 112
Crème de Menthe Punch 119
Frozen Margaritas 114
Frozen Mudslide 118
Hot Buttered Rum 120
Lemony Light Cooler 113
Mai Tai Slush 111
Party Mai Tais 115
Piña Colada 116
Purple Passion 112
Sangria 111
Sangria Blush 114
Shirley Temple 117
Southern Sunshine 110
Spiked Fruit Slush 117
Strawberry Frozen Margaritas 115